Naaman the Syrian

An Examination of the Missionary Work of God in the Life
of Naaman the Syrian as Recorded in 2 Kings 5:1-19

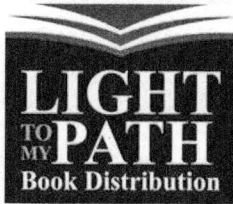

LIGHT TO MY **PATH**
Book Distribution

F. Wayne Mac Leod

Light To My Path Book Distribution
Sydney Mines, Nova Scotia, CANADA
www.lighttomypath.ca

Naaman the Syrian

Copyright © 2020 by F. Wayne Mac Leod

Table of Contents

Preface

This is the story of Naaman, a military commander in the Syrian army. He would be unknown to us but for the grace of Israel's God reaching out to him. Why God touched this man and drew him to Himself is a mystery. Like the apostle Paul, he was an enemy of His people. Like Paul, however, he could not run from the purpose of His Creator.

2 Kings 5:1-19 reveals the heart of God for the nations. It shows us how God pursues those He loves and orchestrates circumstances to bring them to Himself. Naaman did not seek God, but God sought Him and won his heart and devotion.

Namaan's conversion reminds us that God can break even the proudest heart. It shows us that God makes Himself known even to those who are not seeking Him. I trust this study will introduce the reader to Naaman and encourage those whose loved ones have walked away from the Lord and His purpose. May the Lord be pleased to reveal more of Himself and His saving work through this simple study of Naaman the Syrian.

F. Wayne Mac Leod

Chapter 1 - Naaman the Commander

1 Naaman, commander of the army of the king of Syria, was a great man with his master and in high favor, because by him the LORD had given victory to Syria. He was a mighty man of valor, but he was a leper. (2 Kings 5:1)

Let me introduce you to Naaman. He was a Syrian military commander in the king's army. This was an impressive position in itself, but it was not just a title. 2 Kings 5:1 speaks of him as a "great man with his master and in high favour." In other words, he not only fulfilled an important function but excelled as a military commander.

Notice how 2 Kings 5:1 describes Naaman as a "great" man with his master. This tells us that the king highly valued him. His experience, skill and courage were vital assets to the king's army. The fact that he enjoyed "high" favour with the king shows us just how much the king trusted and depended on him.

Naaman obtained this favour and standing, according to 2 Kings 5:1, because of his military victories. He proved himself on the field of battle. He demonstrated that he was a "mighty man of valour" by how he handled himself in warfare. He was a strong and skilled leader. His courage was an inspiration to those who served under his command. He led his soldiers into victory by his brave example.

So far, we have examined 2 Kings 5:1 from a purely human perspective. The verse goes on, however, to give us a glimpse of what was taking place behind the scenes. Notice the phrase, "because of him the LORD had given victory to Syria." If we bypass this thought, we miss the whole point of the story.

Consider this for a moment. Naaman was not an Israelite. He was a commander of an enemy nation. The phrase, "because of him the LORD had given victory to Syria," is perplexing. What is happening here? God is working in the life of an enemy commander, giving him military success. From this, we understand the source of Naaman's victory. He was powerful because the LORD God of Israel was with him. Behind all of this courage and military might was the Lord God of Israel.

Understand here that Naaman did not know or worship the God of Israel, nor did he understand that this God was the source of his victories. The Syrians looked up to Naaman. They did not see the Israelite God as the real power behind their brave commander. Notice the words used to describe Naaman in 2 Kings 5:1:

1. He was "commander of the army of the king of Syria."
2. He was "a great man with his master."
3. He was "in high favour."
4. He was "a mighty man of valour."

All eyes focused on Naaman, and he received credit for his victories. He walked down the street with his head held high. He enjoyed the praise and admiration of the soldiers under him. His country and his king respected him. He was Naaman, the great and mighty man of valour.

While Naaman enjoyed the praise, quietly behind the scenes was a power at work that he did not recognize. The God of Israel had chosen to enable this man. He reached out to him and took a personal interest in him. He decided to bless his efforts and give him victory. Why God chose him is beyond our ability to understand. What is clear is that the Lord God of Israel was interested in revealing Himself even to Israel's Syrian enemies.

We see in 2 Kings 5:1 the heart of God for a Syrian military commander. Even before Naaman had come to know the God of Israel, he experienced His hand on his life. God had a purpose for this military commander.

There is something else we learn about Naaman from 2 Kings 5:1. The verse tells us that Naaman was a leper. Leprosy was a dreaded disease that forced the leper to live in isolation. This illness was a living death for Naaman. It was also a significant loss for the nation and the king's army.

Does it strike you as strange that the verse tells us that God had been giving Naaman victories for Syria but also allowed him to get sick with leprosy? From a purely human perspective, this makes no sense. What good was Naaman as a leper? This leprosy appears to be a hindrance to the victories God was giving him for his nation.

We see from this verse and the context of 1 Kings 5, however, that this leprosy was the means through which Naaman would come to know the Lord God of Israel, who was giving him the victory. From a human perspective, we wonder if God could not have used a less drastic means to introduce Himself to Naaman. Understand, however, the hardness of the human heart and the stubbornness of pride. This leprosy stripped

Naaman of his arrogance and revealed to him the fragility of life. God showed him in those days that as powerful as he felt he was, there was a greater power over which he had no control. Naaman would come to recognize his dependence on God in those days. God forced him to consider the meaning of his life. He would come to understand that he was not in control of his destiny when all his plans could come crashing down on him.

Have you ever been in this situation? Have you ever come to a place of absolute brokenness? We live our lives as if everything depends on us. We rely on our education, our experience, and our skill to carry us through. We rise each morning full of health and energy and return home each evening with provision for our families. We come to trust ourselves but fail to realize that behind all this success is the hand of the God of Israel. Like Naaman, we enjoy health and favour but neglect to understand just how fragile all this can be.

What was it like for Naaman to wake up that morning with leprosy? What was it like to hear that diagnosis and feel at that very instant that his life as he knew it was over? How helpless did he feel that day? That was the day reality struck. He was not in control of his life and future. Everything he had worked for could be taken from him in an instant.

Naaman was a leper. This leprosy, however, would not take his life. Instead, it would be a path that introduced him to the God who had been working in his life, giving him victory and favour with the king and his people. The God who empowered him was getting ready to reveal Himself in a very personal way. As drastic as this leprosy appeared to be, one day, Naaman would look back at this horrible disease with thanksgiving in his heart because it was the means through which he came to know the one true God.

2 Kings 5:1 reveals the great missionary heart of God. We see in this verse how God empowered a Syrian military commander. The God of Israel reached out to this one man in his home in Syria and revealed His power in him. Naaman did not know the God of Israel at this time, but God would introduce Himself in time.

Naaman's leprosy was in the hands of the God of Israel. This illness humbled the valiant military commander and prepared him for what God had in store for his life. God wanted Naaman to know Him. He was softening his heart and humbling him for the time when He would reveal His presence. The pride of Naaman's heart needed to be broken. His ears needed to be opened. Way before Naaman was aware of God, he experienced His work in his life.

As it was for Naaman, God must work in the lives of all who come to Him. Working behind the scenes, God shows His power and humbles those to whom He wishes to introduce Himself. The work of evangelism begins with the work of God in individual lives.

For Prayer:

As we examine this story of Naaman, Father, we see how you chose to work in the most unlikely person. We see your missionary heart. We watch how you began a work in the life of a man who did not know you. You demonstrated your power to Him and then showed him how you could take it all from him in an instant. You humbled his heart through the illness he suffered and prepared him to hear from You.

Father, we have loved ones who need your work. We have shared with them the love of God, but their hearts are not ready to receive this truth. They need your work in them. They need the pride of their heart broken. They need ears to hear what they cannot hear right now. Father, we have no power to convert a soul. Salvation belongs to you alone. Have mercy on our loved ones. As you did for Naaman, begin a deep inner work in their lives so that they can see you and hear your call. Prepare their hearts and introduce Yourself to them.

Chapter 2 - The People God Uses

[2] Now the Syrians on one of their raids had carried off a little girl from the land of Israel, and she worked in the service of Naaman's wife. [3] She said to her mistress, "Would that my lord were with the prophet who is in Samaria! He would cure him of his leprosy."
(2 Kings 5)

The ways of God are often perplexing to us. In the last chapter, we saw how God gave Naaman the Syrian military success and favour with the king and then struck him with leprosy. As we move now to verses two and three of 2 Kings 5, this complexity of God is even more evident.

Verse two begins with a statement about bands of raiding Syrian soldiers.

2 Now the Syrians on one of their raids had carried off a little girl from the land of Israel (2 Kings 5)

Let's take a moment to consider what is happening in this verse. Naaman was a Syrian commander. Verse 2 tells us that his people were raiding the land of Israel. Most commentators agree that the king of Syria did not officially sanction the Syrian raiders here. Instead, they were likely acting out of greed to enrich their own pockets. The fact that verse two uses the phrase "on one of their raids" shows us that this was a regular occurrence. These Syrian bandits made their money by looting and stealing.

Notice in verse two that the Syrians captured a little girl from Israel on one of their raids. The word "little" indicates that this girl was still a child. These raiders would take anything they could use for their profit. The little girl would be sold for a profit when they returned to Syria.

Note that this little Israelite girl worked in the service of Naaman's wife. It is quite likely that Naaman's family purchased her from these Syrian bandits. It was by this means that this Israelite girl came to live in the home of Naaman.

Again, we are left perplexed at the ways of God. Why would He allow a young Israelite girl to be captured and taken from her family and home to work as a slave in Syria? God, however, had a purpose. The presence of this little Israelite girl in the family of Naaman was not without reason.

As this Israelite girl worked in Naaman's home, she became aware of her master's leprosy. His condition weighed on her mind until one day, she approached her mistress and said:

[3] "Would that my lord were with the prophet who is in Samaria! He would cure him of his leprosy." (2 Kings 5)

Let's take a moment to reflect on the words of this young Israelite girl. She was saying something like this: "Oh, how I wish that my master could meet Elisha the prophet. I know he could cure his leprosy." What strikes me here is the great tenderness and compassion of this Israelite slave for her master.

Remember that this young girl had been taken from her homeland and brought to Syria as a slave. She could have been bitter toward the Syrians for selling her as merchandise. They had enriched their pockets at her expense. Instead of bitterness and resentment, her heart broke for her master. She longed to see him recover from his leprosy.

What is behind this compassion? There is only one answer to this question. The Lord God of Israel was working in the heart of this young girl. He had stripped away bitterness, and, in its place, He filled her with forgiveness and empathy toward her master and his condition.

This is not the only thing God was doing in the heart of this little girl, however. Consider the boldness of her statement in verse three. She was a young and inexperienced slave girl. Who was she to approach her mistress and advise her? Why would her mistress even listen to her?

Consider also the faith required to believe that the prophet she spoke about could heal her master. She was telling her mistress that there was a man in Israel who could heal Naaman. She was putting her life on the line here. What would have happened had Naaman gone through the expense of travelling to Israel only to find that this prophet could not or would not heal him. What would be the implications for this little girl if she gave her master false hope and put him through such an expense for nothing?

The words, "*He would cure him of his leprosy,*" are bold words of faith. She risks everything to tell her master about the prophet in Samaria. What is behind these words and demonstrations of faith? Once again, we need to recognize that God has been working in this little Israelite girl. The boldness and confidence she expressed that day were demonstrations of God's work in her heart. God was moving her to step out and speak to her mistress boldly. God had a purpose for Naaman, and this little Israelite girl was part of that purpose.

How easy it would have been for Naaman's wife to brush off what this little girl said that day. What could a little Israelite slave have to say that would be of any interest to her. She was just a little girl. Little girls have all kinds of fanciful ideas not based in reality. There was, however, something about those words that struck Naaman's wife, for the next thing we read is that Naaman is preparing to go to see this Israelite prophet.

We cannot underestimate the working of God in this situation. The words that little girl spoke hit their mark. Naaman's wife could not brush them off. Those words worked on her mind and heart until she knew she had to speak to her husband about them. Such is the power of the word of God. This little Israelite girl would be the instrument of God to speak those words at the right time.

Naaman had many counsellors but not like this young Israelite girl. She did not belong in his council chambers. He would not consult her in times of need. Her advice, however, would prove to be life-changing. God would use this little girl to humble Naaman and set him on a path to healing.

Notice the work of God in the life of Naaman. God empowered him and gave him military success. He also afflicted him with leprosy. Now God orchestrates circumstances so that bands of raiding soldiers capture a particular Israelite girl. God brought those Syrian bandits into contact with Naaman's household when they returned from their raid. Naaman's wife or her servants were in the right place at the right time with the right need and bought this Israelite servant girl. He then emboldens this young girl to share the way of healing and salvation to Naaman. Way before Naaman steps foot on Israelite soil, God was working in his life, preparing him for what He had in store for his life. Do you have a loved one who does not know the Lord? Take courage in what you see in the life of Naaman. God is working behind the scenes.

Another detail we need to see here is in the life of the little Israelite girl. What appeared to be tragic for her proved to be God's way of working out His purpose. God brought this little girl to Syria to speak to Naaman. Yes, there was a sacrifice involved in this —she was taken from her homeland and family. She did not likely understand why she was sold to enrich the pockets of Syrian raiders. God, however, was working in this confusion. God drew near and touched her heart, removing bitterness and anger. In its place, he poured out faith, compassion and love for her master.

The sovereign God of Israel was at work. He chose unlikely people to reveal Himself to Naaman. Leprosy, raiding bands of unruly soldiers out for a quick profit and a little Israelite slave girl, were God's instruments of choice. His ways are very different from ours, but rest assured that though His ways are strange to our eyes, His purpose is clear. He is in the business of revealing Himself to those He loves.

For Prayer

Father, we confess that Your ways are not our ways. You use circumstances and situations we cannot understand to accomplish Your purpose. Thank you for the way you worked in Naaman's life. Thank you for what these verses teach us about how you pursue those you love. As we look at this little Israelite girl's life, we are amazed to see how you used even children to speak to the most influential leaders. Thank you for how You transformed her heart and gave her everything she needed to be Your instrument. Give us the grace to be willing to leave everything just as she did. Where there is unforgiveness in our heart, remove it and replace it with compassion and love. Where there is timidity, replace it with boldness to step out in your leading. Thank you for showing us that you do not need influential and well-educated people to accomplish your purpose. You want men, women, boys and girls who are humble and willing to be used. Thank you that you are eager to equip all who will surrender to You.

Chapter 3 -
The Word of a Servant Girl

[4] So Naaman went in and told his lord, "Thus and so spoke the girl from the land of Israel." [5] And the king of Syria said, "Go now, and I will send a letter to the king of Israel." (2 Kings 5)

Naaman's illness was devastating. Leprosy is a life-changing disease. As a leper, Naaman was isolated from his family and friends. He was not able to perform his duties as a military commander. He could not circulate in the community. He could do nothing about his condition. This great military commander was now fighting a battle he could not win. He was helpless before his disease. He had come to the end of his resources and had to realize that these were forces he could not conquer. God brought Naaman to the end of himself. In his desperation, Naaman would listen to anything or try anything.

In the purpose of God, a little girl came into the home of Naaman, the Syrian. Of all the places this little girl could have been sold, she ended up with Naaman's wife. God overruled even the evil of the Syrian bandits who captured her, so it accomplished His purpose.

We do not know much about this little girl, but the one thing we do know is that God used her in a life-changing way in the life of Naaman. In the last chapter, we saw her faith and the risk she took in telling Naaman's wife about the prophet of Samaria, who could heal her husband's leprosy.

I want to take a moment here to reflect on the power and authority God gave to the words of that little Israelite girl. The words she spoke were simple enough.

[3] She said to her mistress, "Would that my lord were with the prophet who is in Samaria! He would cure him of his leprosy." (2 Kings 5)

In these words, the little girl expressed her wish that Naaman could meet with the prophet of Samaria. She also revealed her belief that he could heal him.

What we need to understand, however, is what God did with those simple words. God empowered the words of that little girl. When she spoke them to Naaman's wife, they burned intensely on her mind. These were words Naaman's wife could not cast off. They offered hope in a desperate time. She did not receive them as the fanciful wishes of a young girl. There was something about these words that demanded action. Naaman's wife felt she had to take what that little girl said and share it with her husband.

When Naaman heard the words, he too took them seriously. Here was a man who was advised by great military men. He took his orders directly from the king. Yet, there was something about the words of that little girl that made his heart beat faster and stirred up his hope. He felt so strongly about what he heard that he determined to speak to the king about it.

Making an appointment with the king of Syria was not something one took lightly. One did not bother royalty with trivial matters. The words of that young girl, however, were so heavy on Naaman's heart that he felt he had to take the king's time to discuss them with him.

With the words of the servant girl heavy on his heart, Naaman sought an audience with the king of Syria. He told the king what she had said:

[4] So Naaman went in and told his lord, "Thus and so spoke the girl from the land of Israel." (2 Kings 5)

Why would Naaman think that the king of Syria would want to hear the words of a little Israelite servant girl? Was this merely a cute story of a little girl's wish for her master? Great military, political and religious leaders advised the king. Why would he be interested in the words of a small foreign girl? Notice, however, the response of the Syrian king:

[5] And the king of Syria said, "Go now, and I will send a letter to the king of Israel." (2 Kings 5)

The words of the Israelite girl also touched the heart of Syria's king. He took what she said so seriously that he wrote an official letter to the king of Israel on Naaman's behalf.

What was it about what that little girl said that moved Naaman and the king of Syria? It is true that she merely expressed her wish that her master meet the Samaritan prophet, but God empowered the words she spoke and gave authority to them. When Naaman and the Syrian king heard them, they knew they needed to respond.

The people of Jesus' day were astonished at the authority with which He spoke:

[28] And when Jesus finished these sayings, the crowds were astonished at his teaching, [29] for he was teaching them as one who had authority, and not as their scribes. (Matthew 7)

The apostle Paul charged Titus to speak with this same authority in Titus 2:15:

[15] Declare these things; exhort and rebuke with all authority. Let no one disregard you. (Titus 2)

The authority the Lord gave to that young Israelite servant girl moved military commanders and kings.

While God empowered the words of the servant girl, what was the attitude of those who heard those words? Admittedly, there is a certain amount of speculation here, but we do understand human nature and know that at this point, neither Naaman, his wife, nor the king had not yet come to know the God of Israel.

Naaman's wife was likely motivated by love for her husband and a desire to have her life return to normal. It would have grieved her to see her husband in his condition.

Naaman was likely thinking of himself as he listened to the words of the servant girl. He, too, wanted to be restored to his family and place in society. It was an embarrassment to be isolated because of leprosy. This humiliation was likely almost too much for him to bear. He probably wanted to be restored to health and position in society.

As for the king, he treasured Naaman as a valued commander. He did not want to lose someone of his stature.

Naaman had given him many victories and enriched his pockets.

Nobody here was thinking of the purpose of God and how to advance the cause of His kingdom. The God of Israel was the furthest thing from their minds. Their motivations for going to see the prophet were likely quite selfish.

There is a strange contrast between the words empowered by God and the selfish motivations of the people who heard those words. They responded, not because the Lord God was speaking to them, but because they saw that there could be some personal benefit from listening.

As we look at the life and ministry of the Lord Jesus, we see how people followed Him not because of the truth He spoke, but because He healed their illnesses. People respond to the Word of God for various reasons. Not all those reasons are honourable. Naaman pursued the advice of the young servant girl, likely for selfish reasons. His heart was changed, however, when he experienced the reality of the words she spoke.

The message of the servant girl set things in motion. When Naaman shared what she had told his wife with the king, the response of the king is interesting:

5 "Go now, and I will send a letter to the king of Israel." (2 Kings 5)

There was no time to waste. "Go now," he said to Naaman. Don't waste another moment. Pack your bags today and go to Israel. Find this prophet and see if he will heal your disease. I will even write a letter to Israel's king requesting that he act on your behalf. Motivated by the servant girl's words and

23

supported by the Syrian king, Naaman packed his bags and travelled to Israel to see if what that little Israelite girl said was true.

Her words were simple, but they were boldly spoken and empowered by God. Ultimately, they would be life-changing for Naaman. Imagine what God could do through you if you were willing to step out boldly like this young Israelite slave.

For Prayer

Father, we see here how you can take the simple things we say and empower them to impact kings and kingdoms. Please give us the boldness and faith of this little Israelite girl. May we speak Your word and step out into Your purpose.

Thank you that while the motivations and intentions of those who respond to Your Word are not always honourable, You still meet them. Thank you for how you transform hearts and minds. Thank you that even before Naaman knew You, You were working in His life, orchestrating circumstances to humble him and bring him to an understanding of who You are. Father, we have loved ones who do not know you. We ask that you work in their lives as well. Empower Your Word. Prepare their lives and hearts to hear and know You.

Chapter 4 -
A Disappointing Testimony

[5] And the king of Syria said, "Go now, and I will send a letter to the king of Israel. So he went, taking with him ten talents of silver, six thousand shekels of gold, and ten changes of clothing. [6] And he brought the letter to the king of Israel, which read, "When this letter reaches you, know that I have sent to you Naaman my servant, that you may cure him of his leprosy." [7] And when the king of Israel read the letter, he tore his clothes and said, "Am I God, to kill and to make alive, that this man sends word to me to cure a man of his leprosy? Only consider, and see how he is seeking a quarrel with me." (2 Kings 5)

With the permission of the king, Naaman quickly prepared his bags for the journey to Israel. Notice what Naaman took with him that day.

Silver and Gold

2 Kings 5:5 tells us that Naaman took ten talents of silver and six thousand shekels of gold. A footnote in the ESV translation of the Bible says this:

A talent was about 75 pounds or 34 kilograms. A shekel was about 2/5 ounce or 11 grams.

According to this, Naaman brought 750 pounds or 340 kilograms of silver and 66,000 grams or 2,328 ounces of gold. At today's rates, the total value of this silver and gold could be up to five million US dollars.

Changes of Clothing

We see also from 2 Kings 5:5 that Naaman also packed ten changes of clothes. These clothes were not for himself. We know this because, in 2 Kings 5:23, Naaman offers two changes of clothes to Elisha's servant. Naaman bought these clothes as gifts. In a culture where many people would not have had a change of clothes, this would have been a wonderful and extravagant gift.

Letter from the king

The final item packed in his bags was a letter from the king of Syria. This letter was addressed to the king of Israel and would have given Naaman safe passage to the king. Remember that Naaman was a leper and, as such, would not be a welcome visitor to Israel. He would not have been able to see the king himself, so this letter was necessary.

What people pack for a trip tells us a lot about them. Naaman's bags show us how rich and influential he was in Syria. What he had to give away was beyond what the average Israelite could even imagine. Naaman's military successes had certainly enriched his pockets.

What we also need to understand is that this wealth would reward those who helped him to recover. Naaman was willing to exchange his wealth for health. He would pay anything to get rid of his leprosy. This disease was so awful that he was ready to part with this great fortune to live a normal life again. Naaman was desperate. He longed to be well.

When Naaman arrived in Israel, he presented the letter to the king. The message read:

> 6 *"When this letter reaches you, know that I have sent to you Naaman my servant, that you may cure him of his leprosy." (2 Kings 5)*

Notice the response of Israel's king to Naaman's letter:

> *[7] And when the king of Israel read the letter, he tore his clothes and said, "Am I God, to kill and to make alive, that this man sends word to me to cure a man of his leprosy? Only consider, and see how he is seeking a quarrel with me."*

Am I God?

The first response of Israel's king is this: *"Am I God, to kill and make alive, that this man sends word to me to cure a man of his leprosy?"* We can understand what the king is saying here. As king, he did not have the power to heal a man of leprosy.

Let's back up for a moment to consider what is happening here. God has been working in the life of Naaman. He gave him great military success. He also humbled him through his leprosy. God also strategically placed a young Israelite girl in his home to direct him to Israel.

27

Naaman was in desperate need of healing. His heart was crying out in despair. He was willing to give his fortune to live a normal life again.

In his desperation, Naaman came to the leader of the people of God and pleaded for help, but that leader could offer him no support. "Am I God that I should heal you," he says. "Why are you coming to me?"

What is striking about this picture is that the king does not even consult God on Naaman's behalf. He does not go to the priests or seek the advice of the prophets. He brushes Naaman off. The king did not have the power to heal leprosy, but he was the leader of a people whose God did great and wonderful things. The history of Israel recounted how their God did cure leprosy and many other diseases. The leader of God's people does not point Naaman to this God.

This picture is sad but often repeated in our day. God regularly sends people like Naaman to us. Indeed, we cannot heal them in our strength, but we do know the God who can. Surely we can point these people to the God of Israel. Surely we can seek Him on their behalf. Sadly, in the case of Naaman, this did not happen.

He is Seeking a Quarrel

Notice the second response of the king of Israel. He accused Syria's king of seeking a quarrel. What was intended as a plea for compassion turned into a political insult. Naaman was charged with a conspiracy to create a political divide. The man who genuinely sought help and healing is condemned as an enemy of Israel seeking to damage Israel and Syria's fragile relations.

Imagine what that day would have been like for Naaman. He had approached the leader of the people of Israel. Their God was the one true God. In Him alone was Naaman's healing found, but he found no support or help.

What kind of testimony was the king of Israel? How well did he represent the intentions and attitude of his God? Instead of consulting God on Naaman's behalf, he brushed him off. Instead of taking him seriously, he accused him of seeking a quarrel.

As we look at these verses, we cannot help but ask ourselves how we would respond in a similar situation. Outside is a leper desperate for healing. At the door is a broken sinner begging for someone to point him to the answer. Down the street is a young mother with nothing left to offer her children. In the back row of your church is a man whose wife is dying of cancer. He has come seeking answers. Will you brush them off with the words: "Am I God that I should heal them?" Will you judge their intentions and accuse them of taking advantage of your goodwill? How will you represent your God before these people?

Naaman's first encounter with the religion of Israel was a bitter one. How disappointed he must have been. The testimony of God's people did not reflect the character and heart of their God. God was working in Naaman's life, but God's people brushed him off and insulted him. That in itself would have been enough to send Naaman back home, but God wasn't finished with him yet.

For Prayer:

Father, you bring people like Naaman to us regularly. They come seeking answers and healing. Forgive us for the times we have not taken them seriously. Please help us to be more in tune with what you are doing and the role you want us to play in the lives of those you put on our path. Forgive us for not representing You and your purpose accurately. Give us greater compassion for those who are suffering in our midst. Give us a heart that will reach out to you on behalf of the suffering and needy.

Chapter 5 -
Elisha's Solution

[8] But when Elisha the man of God heard that the king of Israel had torn his clothes, he sent to the king, saying, "Why have you torn your clothes? Let him come now to me, that he may know that there is a prophet in Israel." [9] So Naaman came with his horses and chariots and stood at the door of Elisha's house. [10] And Elisha sent a messenger to him, saying, "Go and wash in the Jordan seven times, and your flesh shall be restored, and you shall be clean." (2 Kings 5)

We can only imagine how disappointed Naaman was when he came to Israel but found no support. Instead of helping him, Israel's king accused him of seeking a quarrel. What was Naaman to do? Was he to look for the prophet that could heal him, or was he to return home?

As for the king of Israel, he was troubled about this matter. He did not see Naaman as a man seeking help but as one who stirred up trouble between him and Syria. 2 Kings 5:8 tells us that the king of Israel tore his clothes. This was a sign of grief and despair. He, too, did not know what to do. He could not cure Naaman's leprosy, and if he couldn't, he feared the Syrians would invade. He did not want a battle with them.

News travelled to Elisha about Naaman's arrival and the king's response. Hearing this, the prophet sent a word to the king, saying:

8 "Why have you torn your clothes? Let him come now to me, that he may know that there is a prophet in Israel." (2 Kings 5)

There are some critical details in Elisha's words. The first detail relates to the purpose of God for Naaman. When Naaman appeared before the king of Israel, he did not get the response he wanted. The king of Israel misinterpreted Naaman's request and saw him as an enemy seeking a quarrel. That would have been the end of the matter if it were not for the fact that the Lord God had a purpose for Naaman. Yes, the king had failed to be the support Naaman needed, but God wasn't finished with him. God's purpose will not be defeated by unfaithful servants who refuse to recognize it. God moves Elisha to offer a solution, so he wrote, asking the king to send Naaman to him.

The very man Naaman needed sent word to the king to have Naaman come to him. What is interesting about this is the fact that Naaman did not find Elisha by his efforts. God brought Elisha to him. We can only imagine what was going through Naaman's mind when he heard that the prophet the little girl had spoken to him about was reaching out to him. Whether he recognized it or not, this was evidence of the Lord's work in Naaman's life. God was opening doors for him and bringing every circumstance into place for his healing.

There is a second detail we need to see in the words of Elisha to the king. Consider the prophet's question, *"Why have you torn your clothes?* What was Elisha asking here?

To answer this, we need to remind ourselves that Israel served the one true God. This God was the Creator of the world. He chose to reveal Himself to Israel. The history of their nation demonstrated the power of this God. Israel's God promised Abraham's barren wife that He would make a great nation from her descendants. Sarah was in her nineties when she miraculously gave birth to the promised child. When Abraham's descendants were enslaved in Egypt, God raised Moses to set them free. Moses took on the entire nation of Egypt. Through Moses, God broke Israel's bondage and reduced Egypt to nothing. The miracles that took place in the days of Israel's exodus were numerous. Waters parted, rocks yielded water and the desert produced manna for the entire nation to eat. God healed lepers, provided for His people and gave them victory over every enemy. Certainly, the God of Israel was a powerful God to whom nothing was impossible. It is for this reason that the question of Elisha is so important. Why would the king of Israel tear his clothes when he was the king of a nation whose God was so powerful?

The king tore his clothes because he failed to find hope in his God. This was not because God was unwilling to help, but because the king was unable to trust Him in this situation. He lived as if God were not the God of Israel. He didn't trust God.

The problem with the king of Israel is not an isolated one. It is easy to read stories about God in the Bible and not understand that the God we read about is our God as well. We confess that we have a God who is all-powerful and loving, but when we face problems, like the king of Israel, we fail to trust Him. We, too, live as if God were not part of the struggles we encounter. We panic and worry. Do we live as if God did not care for us? The question, "Why have you torn your clothes," is a question we need to ask ourselves in these times. Why do I feel so despairing when the God of Israel has my best interests at heart? Why have I lost all hope when the God who created me and cares deeply for me is in control? In these times, we need to lift our eyes to see God seated on His throne. He is still in control of my life. He still cares for me. There is no reason for despair as long as He reigns.

Notice finally why Elisha asked Naaman to come to him:

Let him come now to me, that he may know that there is a prophet in Israel." (2 Kings 5)

These words express the purpose of God for the life of Naaman. God wanted to reveal Himself to Naaman and brought him to this point in his life for a reason. He stood helplessly before the king of Israel with leprosy, a condition over which he had no control. Naaman was willing to part with his fortune to live a normal life again. He had travelled a long distance seeking an answer. God had humbled him and prepared his heart for this very moment.

Everything was ready now. All that was required was the willingness of a servant to introduce Naaman to the God of Israel. Elisha's words, "that he may know that there is a prophet in Israel," at first glance, may appear to be self-centred. A prophet, however, was the mouthpiece of God. In light of the king's unwillingness to point Naaman to God, Elisha was saying something like this: "Send Naaman to me, so he will know that there is someone who is not afraid to speak to him on God's behalf. I will be God's messenger for him. I will tell him what God wants him to know."

Naaman wasted no time going to see Elisha. Notice what 2 Kings 5:9 tells us:

9 So Naaman came with his horses and chariots and stood at the door of Elisha's house. (2 Kings 5)

Verse nine tells us that Naaman took his horses and chariots with him. These horses and chariots were loaded with gold and silver. By bringing these chariots, Naaman showed Elisha that he would richly reward him if he could heal his leprosy.

Notice the response of Elisha to the presence of Naaman at his door. Verse ten tells us that the prophet sent a messenger to him. That messenger told Naaman to wash in the Jordan River seven times, and he would be cleansed.

Remember that Naaman had leprosy, so Elisha did not personally go to see him. He sent him, instead, to wash in the Jordan River. Despite his leprosy, Naaman was an important man. For Elisha to ignore him like this was insulting.

Naaman came with a great reward for the person who could heal him. He would have praised that person and given him gold and silver in abundance. Elisha was not the healer, however. Why should he be rewarded for what God had done? There are times when we need to get out of the way so that the Lord God alone can receive the glory. This appears to be what is happening here. Elisha points Naaman in the right direction and steps aside. As Naaman obeyed, there would be no human present to credit with the healing. He would realize that his recovery was from the God of Israel alone.

Elisha acted as a messenger and then took a back seat to watch what God would do. That is all God asked him to do. Elisha obeyed God and trusted Him for the results. He stood back so that God could receive all the glory.

One of my great temptations as a servant of God is to go beyond what God has asked me to do. I often feel like I need to be there for the healing or blessing of God's people. I feel the need to be seen as the instrument God uses to restore and strengthen His people. When I do this, however, I take the glory due to God alone for myself. Feeling like I need to be present shows how little I trust God and His ability to change a life without me. This is the height of arrogance. God wants to use me, and for this, I am grateful. When I begin to feel that God cannot accomplish His purpose without me, however, I am overstepping my limit and failing to recognize that God alone is the source of all salvation, healing and refreshing.

By stepping aside, Elisha forces Naaman to look to God alone. The prophet pointed Naaman in the right direction and left him in the hands of God. When he experienced his healing, all glory would go to the Lord God and not to His servant. This must be our great ambition in life as servants of God. We must die to our lust for glory and praise. Our great desire needs to be that God alone receive all praise and honour due to His name.

For Prayer:

Father, we recognize you as the sovereign and all-powerful God who has chosen us to be Your people. Thank you that You care so deeply for us. Forgive us for doubting You. Forgive us for the despair and hopelessness we feel at times. As long as You are our God, we have no cause for fear. You will keep us and supply our needs.

Please give us the grace to be your instruments to point men and women in whom you have been working to Yourself. May we not be ashamed to do so. May we boldly proclaim the power and glory of the God of Israel.

I pray, Lord, that you would help me to understand that You are fully able to renew and heal. May I do what You have called me to do without overstepping my limits. Help me to trust You to do what I cannot do. Teach me how to step back when I need to so that You received all the glory. Forgive me for lusting after the credit that is due only to you. May my greatest delight be in seeing Yu receive all the praise and honour.

Chapter 6 - Naaman's Pride

[11] But Naaman was angry and went away, saying, "Behold, I thought that he would surely come out to me and stand and call upon the name of the LORD his God, and wave his hand over the place and cure the leper. [12] Are not Abana and Pharpar, the rivers of Damascus, better than all the waters of Israel? Could I not wash in them and be clean?" So he turned and went away in a rage. (2 Kings 5)

Naaman's time in Israel was not going as expected. He came with high expectations only to have them dashed. The king of Israel accused him of a conspiracy to cause a quarrel between Israel and Syria. When he went to see Elisha, the prophet sent his messenger instead. As an important official, Naaman was unaccustomed to this kind of treatment. Even though he was a leper, he still had his pride.

Notice the response of Naaman when Elisha refused to see him.

[11] But Naaman was angry and went away, saying, "Behold, I thought that he would surely come out to me (2 Kings 5)

2 Kings 5:11 tells us that Naaman was angry. He expressed the reason for this anger in the first part of verse 11 when he said that he expected Elisha to come out to see him. Imagine

you were a poor beggar in Israel in those days. One day the king of Israel passes by, looks over in your direction but does not speak to you. Will you become angry with him for not talking to you?

As a beggar, you do not expect the king to speak to you. It would surprise you if he did. Your attitude as a beggar is that the king has better things to do than to talk to you. You do not feel you deserve his attention. You do not become angry because you do not expect him to take time for you.

Naaman became angry because he expected Elisha to stop what he was doing to see him. Naaman, unlike the beggar, despite being a leper, felt worthy of Elisha's attention. Remember that he came to the prophet's home with chariots of gold and silver. He had a lot to offer Elisha, and when the prophet did not come to the door, Naaman felt dishonoured. His pride was hurt.

Anger is a natural response when someone hurts our pride. We feel like people are treating us below our dignity. We believe that they owe us respect and feel dishonoured when they don't have the time for us or treat us in a certain way.

Naaman goes on in 2 Kings 5:11 to say that he expected Elisha to:

stand and call upon the name of the LORD his God, and wave his hand over the place and cure the leper. (2 Kings 5)

Naaman expected the prophet to do something particular for him. He hoped not only that Elisha would see him, but that he would also call on the Lord God, wave his hand over his leprosy and cure it. Instead, Elisha told Naaman to wash in the Jordan River. There would be no ceremony or celebration.

40

When Naaman came home from a great victory, people would celebrate that victory. He was used to pomp and celebration. This would not be the case here. No eyes would be on him. Surely, as a great military commander, he deserved something more. There should be some show and excitement. He should be the centre of attention. None of that was going to happen.

Elisha told Naaman to wash seven times in the Jordan River. Notice what Naaman had to say about this in verse 12:

[12] Are not Abana and Pharpar, the rivers of Damascus, better than all the waters of Israel? Could I not wash in them and be clean?" So he turned and went away in a rage. (2 Kings 5)

Naaman was not impressed with the Jordan River. He reminded his servants that there were nicer rivers in Syria. He had been insulted by Elisha and the king of Israel and wanted nothing to do with the Jordan River. His pride welled up in him, and he refused to wash in an Israelite river. He would not humble himself to that point. Verse 12 tells us that he "turned away in a rage." That rage was the result of hurt pride. He believed he was worthy of more respect.

Elisha promised Naaman that if he washed seven times in the Jordan River, he would be healed of his leprosy. The only thing standing between Naaman and his healing was his pride. There was a very intense struggle taking place in Naaman's life. He was a proud man used to special attention. When he spoke, people listened. Wherever he went, people celebrated him and respected him because of his reputation as a great commander. This was not happening in Israel, and he was in a rage.

There are many people like Naaman today. Their pride keeps them from experiencing the fullness of God's blessing. God placed Naaman in a difficult position. On the one hand, there was his need for healing. Leprosy had destroyed his life. Elisha promised healing if he would wash in the Jordan. How could he walk away from this?

Naaman, however, had been insulted and ignored in Israel. Would he listen to those who treated him this way? Would he stoop to wash in an Israelite river for his cure? Were it not for his pride, the answer would have been simple. The man who was willing to part with a fortune in silver and gold to be healed, however, valued his pride more than this great wealth.

Naaman's leprosy did not remove his pride. We should never underestimate the power of pride in our lives. For the sake of his pride, Naaman considered turning his back on the healing he so desperately wanted. He would give up his wealth but not his pride. People worldwide have turned their backs on the salvation of God for the same reason. Former friends have gone to their graves with hurt rather than humble themselves and seek forgiveness. It was this pride that stood between Naaman and his healing. It may be this pride that stands between you and deeper blessing and intimacy with God. Naaman's pride was the dam that blocked all that God wanted to do in him. Until it was broken, that blessing would not flow.

For Prayer:

Father, we see in these verses the power and danger of pride. The example of Naaman is one with which we can all identify.

Naaman's Pride

Any mighty outpouring of blessing is proceeded by a humbling of Your people. We have experienced how pride has kept us from experiencing the fullness of your purpose. Father, show any pride we need to surrender to You today. Give us that grace to humble ourselves before you, for without humility and submission, we will never know the fullness of your blessing. We pray for friends and loved ones whose pride, like that of Naaman, keeps them from what you have for them.

Chapter 7 - Obedience and Healing

[13] But his servants came near and said to him, "My father, it is a great word the prophet has spoken to you; will you not do it? Has he actually said to you, 'Wash, and be clean'?" [14] So he went down and dipped himself seven times in the Jordan, according to the word of the man of God, and his flesh was restored like the flesh of a little child, and he was clean. (2 Kings 5)

In the last chapter, we saw how Naaman "turned and went away in a rage" (2 Kings 5:12). His wounded pride stood in the way of his healing. He would have likely returned home without a cure were it not for one of his servants who challenged him to reconsider the words of the prophet.

There is something else worth mentioning here about the pride of Naaman. Consider what Naaman's servant told him in verse 13:

"My father, it is a great word the prophet has spoken to you; will you not do it? Has he actually said to you, 'Wash, and be clean'?" (2 Kings 5)

Naaman's servant reminded his master of what Elisha told him. We will come back to this in a moment. What is important for us to note here is that Naaman did not hear what Elisha said.

When Elisha did not even greet Naaman and told him to wash in the Jordan River, Naaman's pride was hurt. His hurt pride deafened his ears to what the prophet said to him that day. Elisha spoke to him about healing for his leprosy, but that was not what he heard. He heard Elisha say something like this: "I don't have time for you, so I am sending my servant. Just wash in the Jordan River." The words Naaman heard made him angry, and he left Elisha's home in a rage.

It was a wise servant who boldly spoke to Naaman and helped him to see reason. Speaking to his master, the servant said: "My Father, it is a great word the prophet has spoken to you" (2 Kings 5:13). Naaman needed this reminder. He wasn't thinking straight. His pride was in the way, and he needed someone with a clear mind to show him what Elisha had told him. Notice the words of the servant in 2 Kings 5:13 to Naaman: "Has he said to you, 'Wash, and be clean?'" "Master," the servant told Naaman, "the prophet of Israel said that if you washed, you would be healed. That is excellent news." Notice the challenge of the servant in 2 Kings 5:13 – "will you not do it?" It wasn't until that servant helped him see what Elisha said that Naaman was willing to wash in the Jordan River.

How easy it is for us to hear what we want to hear. Many things affect our ability to understand what someone says to us. In Naaman's case, his hurt pride deafened his ears to the incredible words of Elisha. The experiences of our past can shape how we hear things today. Maybe you have had a bad experience with believers who were not living as they should. That has now affected how you respond to other believers. You are no longer open to what they say because of your experience. Our hurts, prejudices, or insecurities will affect how we hear. Elisha told Naaman how to be healed, but he missed it and heard something else. Don't miss out on the truth because your pride or prejudice deafens you.

If Naaman was going to hear the truth Elisha spoke, he would have to stop listening to his wounded pride. God gave him another chance through his servant, who helped him see what his pride would not let him see.

Convinced by his servant, Naaman decided to listen to the words of Elisha. He went to the Jordan River to wash seven times. There is no evidence in the passage that he had faith in the God of Israel. Naaman, to this point, never professed to worship Israel's God. The last word we have about him was that he was angry and in a rage.

While there is no evidence in the passage of faith before washing in the Jordan, what we do have is an act of obedience. There are times when we don't have faith to believe that God will do something. In those times, all we can do is obey what we believe God is asking us to do. While Naaman may not have had faith in the God of Israel, he did finally obey. That is all God required. It was obedience that opened the door to his healing.

After washing seven times, as Elisha told him, Naaman came up out of the water completely restored. 2 Kings 5:14 tells us:

14 and his flesh was restored like the flesh of a little child, and he was clean. (2 Kings 5)

Notice that his skin was like that of a small child. In other words, it was soft and clear. It was better than it had been before his leprosy. God didn't just restore him to his former condition –He made him better than he had ever been.

47

In 2 Kings 5:13-14, we have a picture of a man whose prided deafened his ears so that he did not hear what the prophet of God was telling him. He interpreted Elisha's words through the filter of his pride and prejudice. The filters of our past experiences and hurts can keep us from the truth. If we want to know the truth, we must be willing to listen without prejudice and preconceived ideas. Listen to the response of Natanael when Philip told him about the Lord Jesus:

[46] Nathanael said to him, "Can anything good come out of Nazareth?" Philip said to him, "Come and see." (John 1)

Philip told Natanael to put aside his prejudice and come with him to see for himself. Natanael's preconceptions were shattered that day, and he understood Jesus to be indeed the Son of God. May God give us the grace to listen with fresh ears.

These verses also show us the importance of obedience. Naaman's faith in the God of Israel was questionable, but God healed him because he obeyed. His obedience may not have been the fruit of genuine faith and love. His servant convinced him to do what the prophet told him to do. He may still have had a negative attitude toward Israel, and he had not resolved his conflict with its king and prophet. This weak obedience, however, was all God required. By stepping into the Jordan River, Naaman unleashed the healing power of God. He went into that river a leper with a lot of unresolved issues. He would not come out the same.

God is not looking for perfect people to come to him. We all step into the river of His healing and forgiveness, broken and wounded. Naaman needed healing of his heart as well as healing of the body. Listen to what the Lord God is saying to you. Come as you are with all your hurts. Obey what He is telling you. You may not have the faith to believe, but you can obey. That is what Naaman did, and God not only met him that day but healed him as well. He would never be the same after that encounter.

For Prayer:

Father, as we consider the words of 2 Kings 5:13-14, we recognize that many things can keep us from hearing what you are saying to us. Remove the pride and prejudice that blocks our ears. Heal the hurt that deafens us and keeps us from listening. Please give us the grace to truly hear what you are saying to us. Don't let us walk away from our healing because we cannot lay down our pride, prejudice and hurt.

Lord, we confess that there are times when we do not have the faith to believe what you are saying. In those times, please give us the willingness to obey anyway. Thank you that obedience releases the floodgates of your grace and places us on the path of healing.

Thank you that we do not have to be perfect to experience Your grace. We come wounded and sick. We come with little or no faith, but You touch all who will listen and obey.

Chapter 8-
A Changed Life

[15] Then he returned to the man of God, he and all his company, and he came and stood before him. And he said, "Behold, I know that there is no God in all the earth but in Israel; so accept now a present from your servant." [16] But he said, "As the LORD lives, before whom I stand, I will receive none." And he urged him to take it, but he refused.
(2 Kings 5)

Being convinced by his servant to do as Elisha the prophet had said, Naaman washed in the Jordan River. The result was that he was healed of his leprosy. 2 Kings 5:15 tells us that after his healing:

15 he returned to the man of God, he and all his company, and he came and stood before him. (2 Kings 5)

The words are easy enough to understand, but we need to see them in the context of Naaman's last contact with Elisha. 2 Kings 5:11 tells us that in the previous encounter between these two men, "Naaman was angry and went away." Consider what it would have been like for Naaman to return to Elisha after being so angry with him.

Returning to the man of God required humbling himself and recognizing he was wrong. He stood before the prophet, ashamed that he had been so angry and frustrated with him. God was dealing with Naaman's pride here.

As Naaman stood before Elisha, the anger and bitterness were transformed into gratitude. He came now to offer his thanks to Elisha and confess his change of heart. The proud Naaman now bows before the servant of God in humble appreciation. He declares deep thankfulness to the one who had offended him. In this, we see a humbling of Naaman's heart.

The change in Naaman is not only reflected in a more humble attitude but also in what he said to Elisha that day:

15 Behold, I know that there is no God in all the earth but in Israel (2 Kings 5)

Naaman was a Syrian military commander. In 2 Kings 5:18, we read that he would go with his master to worship the god Rimmon. The words he speaks here are quite powerful. In saying that, there was no God in all the earth, but in Israel, Naaman was renouncing his Syrian gods. Remember that Naaman was not alone when he went to see Elisha. He went with "all his company" (2 Kings 15:15). Before this company of Syrians, Naaman declared that all gods apart from the God of Israel were false. These were bold words, but Naaman recognized that he owed his life to the God of Israel who had healed him.

Notice the words "I know" in verse 15. These words leave little room for doubt. The God of Israel had revealed Himself to Naaman in a life-changing way. He had demonstrated not only His power to heal but also His interest in Naaman personally. Never had a god touched him in this way or shown such a concern for him and his pain.

In 2 Kings 5:15, Naaman wanted to express his gratitude by offering a gift to Elisha. It was only natural for Naaman to feel this way. He was grateful and wanted to reward those who had were involved in his healing. Even though he urged Elisha to accept his gift, the prophet refused, saying:

16 *"As the LORD lives, before whom I stand, I will receive none." (2 Kings 5)*

Elisha does not explain why he refused Naaman's gift. While we can only speculate about his reasons, there are several details we need to consider.

Consider the Gift Naaman Brought

As Naaman prepared to go to Israel, he brought with him a vast fortune. The chariots parked in Elisha's yard were loaded with gold and silver. Naaman's healing meant so much to him that he was willing to part with his great fortune. Naaman's gift to Elisha would have made him a very wealthy man.

Consider What this Gift Would have Done

Consider next what this gift of Naaman would have done. Present with Elisha that day was his servant Gehazi. Gehazi heard his master refuse the gift offered. When Naaman left the presence of Elisha, Gehazi said to himself:

[20] "See, my master has spared this Naaman the Syrian, in not accepting from his hand what he brought. As the LORD lives, I will run after him and get something from him." (2 Kings 5)

When Gehazi caught up with Naaman, he made up a story about Elisha receiving guests and wanting to bless them. He asked Naaman if he would give him something for these guests. Naaman gave him two changes of clothes and two talents of silver. A talent is equal to seventy-five pounds or thirty-four kilogrammes. This means that Naaman gave Gehazi one hundred and fifty pounds or sixty-eight kilogrammes of silver. The value of one pound of silver at the time of writing is about $US 291. In today's market, this gift would have been worth $US 43,650. He also got two changes of clothes in this transaction.

The temptation for Gehazi was too much. He could not stand by and watch such a fortune pass by. His greed got the best of him, and he deceived Naaman to get his hands on some of his fortune. When Elisha discovered what had happened, he told Gehazi that Naaman's leprosy would forever cling to him and his descendants.

The amount of money Naaman wanted to offer Elisha would have changed his life. God had called the prophet to a particular lifestyle. Naaman's gift would have changed that and become a snare for the prophet. This fortune would bring with it many distractions and temptations. Elisha valued his calling more than the wealth Naaman offered him. He chose to live a life free from the distractions of money and possessions.

How many servants of God have fallen prey to the temptations of materialism? Gehazi, Elisha's servant, fell into this temptation. Elisha would not consider it.

Consider What Offering this Gift Would Have Said to Naaman

Consider finally what this gift would have said to Naaman. Had he made Elisha a wealthy man, he would have gone home feeling like he had paid for his healing. God and His blessings are not bought or sold.

In Acts 8, we have the story of Simon, the magician. When he saw that God gave the Holy Spirit through the laying on of the apostles' hands, he offered to pay them to give him this power. Listen to the response of Peter to his request:

[20] But Peter said to him, "May your silver perish with you, because you thought you could obtain the gift of God with money! [21] You have neither part nor lot in this matter, for your heart is not right before God. [22] Repent, therefore, of this wickedness of yours, and pray to the Lord that, if possible, the intent of your heart may be forgiven you. (Acts 8)

Peter rebuked Simon because he believed that he could obtain the gift of God with money. He told him that his heart was not right and that he needed to repent. God's blessings are offered freely because He is a gracious God.

We depreciate the grace and mercy of God when we feel that it can be purchased or earned. There is not a single gift that we deserve. God is not influenced or attracted by our money. His favour cannot be bought or sold like a corrupt judge.

There is one further point we need to make here about Elisha's refusal to receive Naaman's gift. Had Elisha accepted Naaman's offer, the attention would have been on the prophet and not on the God who healed. Elisha's role was to be a messenger. God did the healing. If I tell someone about a doctor who can operate on them and cure their condition, should I be rewarded instead of the doctor when that person is well again?

By refusing to accept Naaman's gift, Elisha recognized that he was not Naaman's healer. The God of Israel alone deserved all the praise. Naaman returned home, his fortune still intact, knowing that the God of Israel had graciously and freely met him and healed his leprosy.

For Prayer

Father God, thank you for what you did in the life of Naaman. Thank you for his physical healing. Thank you that you also transformed an angry and bitter man into one who was grateful for his recovery. Thank you that you stripped away the pride of his heart and allowed him to stand humbly before the one who offended him. Thank you that you removed the doubt in Naaman's mind and assured him that there was no true God but the God of Israel.

Lord, we see how willing Naaman was to part with his wealth in gratefulness for his healing. We also know the temptation that wealth was for Elisha's servant. Please give us the ability to be content with what you have given us. Keep us from the snare of materialism. Protect us from the sinful attractions of this world.

Help us to remember that you alone are worthy of all praise and thanksgiving. Teach us to live and serve in such a way that you receive all glory.

Chapter 9 -
Life as a Believer in
Israel's God

[17] Then Naaman said, "If not, please let there be given to your servant two mule loads of earth, for from now on your servant will not offer burnt offering or sacrifice to any god but the LORD. [18] In this matter may the LORD pardon your servant: when my master goes into the house of Rimmon to worship there, leaning on my arm, and I bow myself in the house of Rimmon, when I bow myself in the house of Rimmon, the LORD pardon your servant in this matter." [19] He said to him, "Go in peace." (2 Kings 5)

When Naaman met the God of Israel, his life was forever changed. His declaration, "Behold, I know that there is no God in all the earth but in Israel," shows that he recognized only one true God. He chose from that point forward to worship the God of Israel.

2 Kings 5:17-18 shows us something of Naaman's commitment to this God of Israel. In these verses, he speaks to Elisha about two matters on his mind as he returned to Syria as a worshipper of Israel's God.

Two Mule Loads of Israel's Earth

The first matter of concern for Naaman, in verse 17, is related to the worship of Israel's God in his homeland.

[17] Then Naaman said, "If not, please let there be given to your servant two mule loads of earth, for from now on your servant will not offer burnt offering or sacrifice to any god but the LORD.

In verse 17, Naaman requested two mule loads of earth, promising never to bring an offering or sacrifice to any god but the Lord God of Israel. This commitment to worship only the God of Israel was powerful. Remember that the Syrians had their gods. Naaman would stand out in his homeland for his refusal to worship these national gods. He might even find himself in trouble because of his commitment to Israel's God. How could a respected Syrian military commander ally himself with the God of another nation?

We are also left wondering what would happen in his family as he returned to introduce them to the God of Israel and His ways. What would his wife and extended family think? Would they follow Naaman in his commitment, or would they shun him? Naaman did not have answers to these questions, but he determined that his loyalty would be to Israel's God no matter what happened. We have to admire this courage.

As if to seal his commitment to the God of Israel, Naaman requested permission to take two mule loads of earth from Israel back to Syria. The request is connected with his desire to offering burnt offerings and sacrifices to the Lord God of Israel alone. To understand what Naaman is saying here, we need to examine Exodus 20:24, where God speaks to His people about building altars:

[24] An altar of earth you shall make for me and sacrifice on it your burnt offerings and your peace offerings, your sheep and your oxen. In every place where I cause my name to be remembered I will come to you and bless you. (Exodus 20)

Notice that God asked his people to build an altar for burnt offerings out of earth. What Naaman seems to be saying is that when he returned to Syria, he was going to make an altar of earth according to the standards set out by the law of Moses. He would then bring his offerings and sacrifices to the Lord on this altar.

Naaman does not say why he chose to use Israel's earth to make this altar. Bible scholars have offered many different suggestions. Some suggest that Naaman felt that he could only worship God on Israelite soil. Others suggest that he asks Elisha for this earth to have his blessing on the construction of an altar for the worship of God in Syria. Maybe he felt that the soil of Syria was unworthy of the God of Israel. We do not have any indication in the passage of Naaman's motivation and intention. What is important is that we understand his purpose. He was going to build an altar from the soil of Israel to worship the one true God who had healed him. His commitment was to that God alone.

When Naaman came to know the Lord God of Israel, he determined to break with his former gods. He would not add the God of Israel to his list of gods to worship. He would not return to his former gods. Naaman's life changed when he met Israel's God. He returned to Syria with many questions on his mind. Would his family accept his new-found faith in Israel's God? How would this change his relationships with friends and co-workers? He did not have an answer to these questions, but he committed himself to follow through with his new faith in God.

Rimmon

The second issue that concerned Naaman as he returned to Syria as a believer in the God of Israel had to do with the practice of going to the house of Rimon, the Syrian god.

[18] In this matter may the LORD pardon your servant: when my master goes into the house of Rimmon to worship there, leaning on my arm, and I bow myself in the house of Rimmon, when I bow myself in the house of Rimmon, the LORD pardon your servant in this matter." [19] He said to him, "Go in peace." (2 Kings 5)

At first glance, Naaman seems to say that when he returned to Syria, he would go to the temple of the pagan god Rimmon and bow down to him. It also appears that he is asking Elisha for forgiveness in advance for this sin he would commit on purpose. The response of Elisha in verse 19 was to offer this forgiveness by telling him to "Go in peace." We need to interpret this verse, however, in the context of the whole passage. We need to address a few issues if we are going to understand what Naaman is telling Elisha here.

First, remember the words of Naaman to Elisha in verse 17:

from now on, your servant will not offer burnt offering or sacrifice to any god but the LORD. (2 Kings 5:17)

Naaman made it his commitment to worship no other god but the God of Israel. If Naaman is telling Elisha in verses 18-19 that he would worship Rimmon on his return, he would be contradicting himself and going against his promise to Elisha.

The second issue we need to examine comes in the response of Elisha. Elisha told Naaman to "go in peace." If Naaman were telling Elisha that he was going to bow down to Rimmon, the prophet could hardly pardon such a serious offence. Nor would the prophet condone a sin that Naaman was purposefully planning to commit. Can you imagine someone going to God and saying: "God, I am going to turn my back on you and commit a great sin, so I am asking you to forgive me in advance because I don't want to be held responsible for what I am going to do"?

The website BiblicalHebrew.org posted an article about tenses in the Hebrew language of Bible times.

The name 'tenses' as applied to Hebrew verbs is misleading. The so-called Hebrew' tenses' do not express the time but merely the state of an action. Indeed were it not for the confusion that would arise through the application of the term 'state' to both nouns and verbs,' states' would be a far better designation than 'tenses.' It must always be borne in mind that it is impossible to translate a Hebrew verb into English without employing a limitation (viz. of time) which is entirely absent in the Hebrew. The ancient Hebrews never thought of an action as past, present, or future, but simply as perfect, i.e. complete, or imperfect, i.e. as in course of development. When we say that a certain Hebrew tense corresponds to a Perfect, Pluperfect, or Future in English, we do not mean that the Hebrews thought of it as Perfect, Pluperfect, or Future, but merely that it must be so translated in English. The time of an action the Hebrews did not attempt to express by any verbal form.

https://biblicalhebrew.org/hebrew-tenses.aspx#:~:text=The%20so-called%20Hebrew%20'tenses,the%20state%20of%20an%20action.&text=of%20time)%20which%20is%20entirely,as%20in%20course%20of%20development

This article tells us that the Hebrew language of the Jewish Scriptures do not reflect past, present or future actions as we do in many languages today. This fact has led some Bible commentators to believe that Naaman was not planning to sin against the God of Israel by bowing down to a pagan god but rather confessing his past sin. Adam Clarke, commenting on this passage, says:

2Ki 5:18 It is useless to enter into the controversy concerning this verse. By no rule of right reasoning, nor by any legitimate mode of interpretation, can it be stated that Naaman is asking pardon for offenses which he may commit, or that he could ask or the prophet grant indulgence to bow himself in the temple of Rimmon, thus performing a decided act of homage, the very essence of that worship which immediately before he solemnly assured the prophet he would never practice. The original may legitimately be read, and ought to be read, in the past, and not in the future tense. "For this thing the Lord pardon thy servant, for that when my master Hath Gone into the house of Rimmon to worship there, and he Hath Leaned upon mine hand, that I also Have Bowed myself in the house of Rimmon; for my worshipping in the house of Rimmon, the Lord pardon thy servant in this thing." This is the translation of Dr. Lightfoot, the most able Hebraist of his time in Christendom.

Life as a Believer in Israel's God

Clarke, Adam, Commentary on the Bible by Adam Clarke [1831]: L A R I D I A N, Marion, Iowa

John Gill states much the same in his Bible commentary when he interprets 2 Kings 5:18 as follows:

his request to the prophet, or to the Lord, is, not for pardon for a sin to be committed; nor to be indulged in his continuance of it; not to worship the idol along with his master; nor to dissemble the worship of it, when he really worshipped it not; nor to be excused any evil in the discharge of his post and office; but for the pardon of the sin of idolatry he had been guilty of, of which he was truly sensible, now sincerely acknowledges, and desires forgiveness of; and so Dr. Lightfoot {w}, and some others {x}, interpret it; and to this sense the words may be rendered, when my master went in to the house of Rimmon to worship there; which was his usual custom; and he leaned on my hand, which was the common form in which he was introduced into it: and I worshipped in the house of Rimmon, as his master did, for the same word is used here as before; in as much, or seeing I have worshipped in the house of Rimmon, have been guilty of such gross idolatry: the Lord, I pray, forgive thy servant in this thing; the language of a true penitent.

Gill, John, John Gill's Exposition of the Entire Bible, L A R I D I A N: Cedar Rapids, Iowa

If what these commentators say is true, then Naaman is not telling Elisha that he was going to sin against God. Instead, he confesses his past sin of worshipping Rimmon, the Syrian god and is asking for forgiveness. He was now renouncing this god and making it his commitment to worship only the

God of Israel. By taking back two mule loads of Israelite soil, he told Elisha that this was the only place he would worship from that point forward. Knowing the sincerity of Naaman's heart, Elisha sends him home with his blessing, "Go in peace."

As we look at the life of Naaman, we see how God took a pagan Syrian military officer who worshipped the god Rimmon and transformed his life. God was working in Naaman's life before Naaman even knew Him. He blessed Naaman's military career and gave him great favour. When Naaman contracted leprosy, God brought a little Israelite girl to his house. She spoke to Naaman's wife about the prophet Elisha. When Naaman heard of this prophet, he was compelled to go to Israel.

Taking a massive fortune with him, the Syrian military officer went to see the king of Israel. Israel's king accused him of trying to start a quarrel between the two countries. When he went to see Elisha, the prophet offended him by refusing to come out to see him. Naaman's pride was hurt, and he would have returned to his homeland bitter and leprous were it not for the advice of a servant who challenged him to listen to the words of Elisha.

Naaman's healing changed his life. The God of Israel became very real to him that day. He broke with all other gods and decided to serve the one true God of Israel. We do not know how things turned out for Naaman when he returned to Syria. The story of Naaman shows us God's heart for the world. He reached out to a single person in Syria. Naaman was not seeking God, but God was undoubtedly seeking him. God orchestrated the events of his life so that Naaman came to know Him as the one true God.

The story of Naaman, the Syrian, is a story of God's grace and sovereign working in individual lives. It is an account of how the God of Israel pursued a lost sheep. It reminds us that God sees those who are his and chases after them until He wins their heart. Naaman's life was changed not because he was seeking the God of Israel but because the God of Israel sought Him.

Ultimately this is our story as well. The God of Naaman also pursued us. He sovereignly brought people and circumstances into our lives that would point us to Him. Like Naaman, many of us came to know the Lord God of Israel when we were still full of pride and anger. God broke through, however, and our lives were forever changed. How we need to thank Him that He did not give up His pursuit but persevered in us until we saw Him as the one and only God deserving of our praise and service.

For Prayer

Father, thank you for the way you worked in the life of Naaman. You changed the life of an enemy of Israel and brought him into submission to you and Your purpose. Thank you for the people and circumstances you brought into my life to bring me to Yourself. May I, like Naaman, commit myself to worship only You. May I never lose sight of what You have done in me. May my heart be eternally devoted to You alone.

Light To My Path Book Distribution

Light To My Path Book Distribution (LTMP) is a book writing and distribution ministry reaching out to needy Christian workers in Asia, Latin America, and Africa. Many Christian workers in developing countries do not have the resources necessary to obtain Bible training or purchase Bible study materials for their ministries and personal encouragement.

F. Wayne Mac Leod is a member of Action International Ministries and has been writing these books with a goal to distribute them freely to needy pastors and Christian workers around the world.

These books are being used in preaching, teaching, evangelism and encouragement of local believers in over sixty countries. Books have now been translated into several languages. The goal is to make them available to as many believers as possible.

The ministry of LTMP is a faith-based ministry, and we trust the Lord for the resources necessary to distribute the books for the encouragement and strengthening of believers around the world. Would you pray that the Lord would open doors for the translation and further distribution of these books? For more information about Light To My Path Book Distribution visit our website at www.lighttomypath.ca

Printed in Great Britain
by Amazon

85394365R00041